*D*ESIGNED AND EDITED BY

REATA STRICKLAND

THE FREE PRESS

NEW YORK LONDON TORONTO SYDNEY SINGAPORE

*f*P

THE FREE PRESS
A Division of Simon & Schuster, Inc.
1230 Avenue of the Americas
New York, NY 10020

Design and editing copyright © 2001
by Reata Strickland

All rights reserved, including the right of
reproduction in whole or in part in any form.

THE FREE PRESS and colophon are
trademarks of Simon & Schuster, Inc.

For information about special discounts
for bulk purchases, please contact
Simon & Schuster Special Sales: 1-800-456-6798
or business@simonandschuster.com

Manufactured in the United States of America

10   9   8   7   6   5   4   3   2   1

Library of Congress Cataloging-in-Publication
Data is available

ISBN 0-7432-2957-6

TO MY
FAITHFUL
FRIEND

ACKNOWLEDGMENTS

To Steve, Jessie, and Katie for your loving support. To Linda, Tonya, and Priscilla for your comforting words of encouragement. To Lennie, Sam, and Jim for keeping my feet on the ground. And to Mother, Kathy, Renea, Ron, and Glenda.

INTRODUCTION

*A*ll my life I have heard stories of how God can use anyone. Anyone. There was Moses, the chronic stutterer who spoke purposefully and beautifully for the release of the Israelites. There was Zacchæus, the ruthless tax collector who learned forgiveness and generosity. There was Mary Magdalene, a prostitute who discovered the power of starting over and the compassion that comes in such a transformation. But never, ever was there a Reata, an artist in Tuscaloosa, Alabama, who used the Internet to reach millions with a message of hope and faith.

In the summer of 2001, I spent a couple of days developing an on-line presentation, *Interview with God*. The words had touched me years earlier, and I vowed to do something with them someday. I finished the presentation and uploaded it to a Web site, pleased that I had finally made good on my promise. Four days later, I received word that half a million people had viewed the site, and that it would be shut down because of the high traffic. I ended up hosting the presentation on my own Web site, reata.org, where millions have viewed it and passed it on to their friends and family. Some of them have translated it into many different languages. I began to receive hundreds of e-mails daily from people all over the world who wanted to express their appreciation, share their beliefs, and tell their individual stories.

Several people have asked why I put the presentation together, and I tell them I created it because I know its message is true. I know the person about whom it was written. His voice is unmistakable. His words speak to a deep place within me, and they bring life. He can heal, encourage, counsel, and cause a change in anyone who will allow His Spirit to work in them.

As a child in Bible school, I heard stories about people who spoke to God face-to-face and shared meaningful relationships with Him. Why were such relationships no longer commonplace? I assumed that our distance was spatial, determined by the course of history rather than the course of a life. Now I am not so sure. Perhaps these relationships are still common, and the only difference is that everyone except me is too skeptical to give them credence. I can only point out that someone wrote *Interview with God*, and somehow it has touched the lives of millions.

The beauty of *Interview with God* arises from the startling contrast between the flaws of humanity and the powerful love of God, a love that is not ignorant of our nature, but stronger than any of our weaknesses. The interview shows that God is quite aware, even if we are not, of our discontent, ignorance, failures, unforgivingness, and self-doubt, and I guess just about everyone can find comfort in that.

Recently, over lunch, I told a friend about the whole experience, about the phone calls and the e-mails, about the record number of visits to the Web site, about such a small thing becoming so big. *Interview with God* did not begin as my most important work, I told her. It was by no means the biggest project I've worked on. It wasn't the most difficult or the most challenging. She stopped me: "But it was enough." And so it was.

I didn't write the words to the *Interview with God*. I didn't take the photos that accompany those words in the on-line presentation. I just put them together and made them available for anyone who needed them, anyone who could be touched by them. So now, I share them again, in a different form, hoping that you, too, will find the everlasting peace and eternal "enoughness" of our Creator.

INTERVIEW
WITH GOD

I DREAMED I HAD AN
INTERVIEW WITH GOD.

"SO YOU WOULD LIKE TO INTERVIEW ME?" GOD ASKED.

"IF YOU HAVE
THE TIME,"
I SAID.

GOD SMILED,

"MY TIME IS ETERNITY."

"WHAT QUESTIONS DO YOU HAVE IN MIND FOR ME?"

"WHAT SURPRISES YOU MOST ABOUT HUMANKIND?"

GOD ANSWERED...

"THAT THEY GET BORED WITH CHILDHOOD.

THEY RUSH TO GROW
UP AND THEN LONG TO
BE CHILDREN AGAIN."

"THAT THEY LOSE
THEIR HEALTH TO
MAKE MONEY

AND THEN
LOSE THEIR MONEY TO
RESTORE THEIR HEALTH."

"THAT BY THINKING
ANXIOUSLY ABOUT
THE FUTURE,

THEY FORGET
THE PRESENT,

SUCH THAT THEY
LIVE IN NEITHER
THE PRESENT NOR
THE FUTURE."

"THAT THEY LIVE
AS IF THEY WILL
NEVER DIE,

AND DIE AS IF THEY
HAD NEVER LIVED."

GOD'S HAND
TOOK MINE
AND WE WERE
SILENT FOR
A WHILE.

AND THEN I ASKED...

"As a parent,
what are
some of life's
lessons you
want your
children to
learn?"

GOD REPLIED
WITH A SMILE,

"To learn
they cannot
make anyone
love them.

WHAT THEY CAN DO
IS LET THEMSELVES
BE LOVED. "

"TO LEARN THAT IT IS NOT GOOD TO COMPARE THEMSELVES TO OTHERS."

"To learn that
a rich person
is not one who
has the most,

BUT IS ONE WHO
NEEDS THE LEAST."

"TO LEARN THAT
IT TAKES ONLY A FEW
SECONDS TO OPEN
PROFOUND WOUNDS IN
PERSONS WE LOVE,

AND IT TAKES MANY YEARS
TO HEAL THEM."

"TO LEARN
TO FORGIVE
BY PRACTICING
FORGIVENESS."

"TO LEARN THAT THERE ARE PERSONS WHO LOVE THEM DEARLY,

BUT SIMPLY DO NOT KNOW
HOW TO EXPRESS OR SHOW
THEIR FEELINGS. "

"TO LEARN THAT
TWO PEOPLE CAN LOOK
AT THE SAME THING
AND SEE IT
DIFFERENTLY."

"TO LEARN THAT IT IS NOT
ALWAYS ENOUGH THAT THEY
BE FORGIVEN BY OTHERS.

THEY MUST FORGIVE
THEMSELVES."

"And to learn
that I am here